**Fill in the speech bubble below in your best handwriting.**

My name is _____

My favourite toy is _____

My favourite food is _____

D0995715

**Fill in the lines below when you have finished the book.**
**Look at how much your writing has improved!**

My name is _____

My favourite toy is _____

My favourite food is _____

1

# Lower Case Letters 1

Meet the first letter family! Trace and write the letters by starting at the red dots and following the arrows.

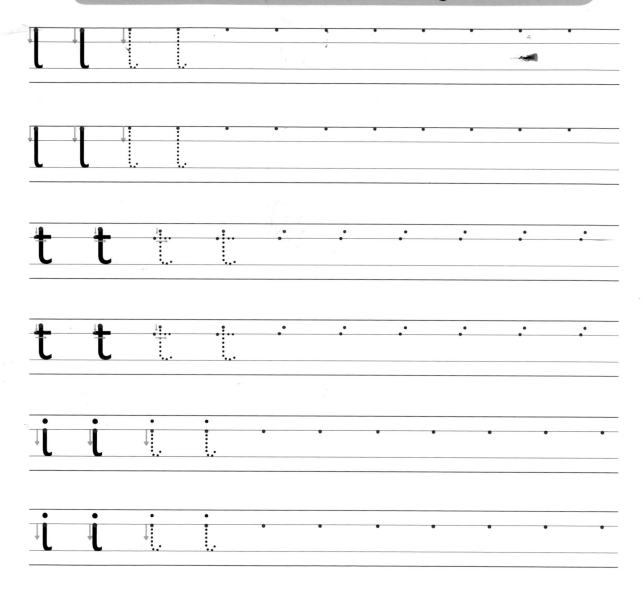

I'm a terrific telescope!

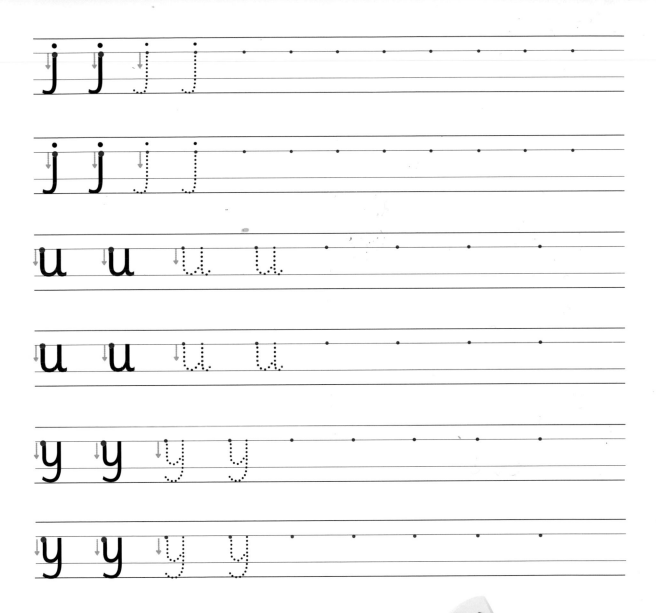

j j j j

j j j j

u u u u

u u u u

y y y y

y y y y

3

# Lower Case Letters 2

Here's your second letter family! Trace and write the letters.

a a a a · · · · ·

a a a a · · · · ·

c c c c · · · · · ·

c c c c · · · · · ·

d d d · · · · · ·

d d d · · · · · ·

I'm an awesome alien!

STAR TIP!
All these letters start near the top of the curve and then go up, round and down. Follow the arrows!

g g g g

g g g g

o o o o

o o o o

q q q q

q q q q

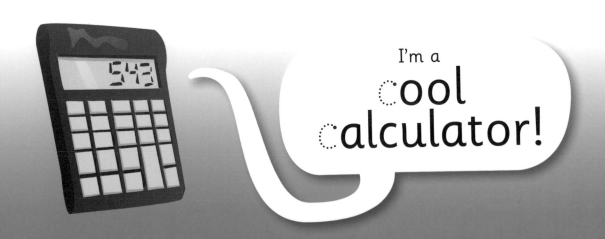

543

I'm a
cool
calculator!

5

Have fun with letter family 3! Trace and write the letters.

r r r r

r r r r

b b b b

b b b b

h h h h

h h h h

We are
brilliant
balloons!

STAR TIP!
To write these letters, start at the top, then go down and then go back up again. Follow the arrows!

6

m m m m

m m m m

n n n n

n n n n

p p p p

p p p p

k k k k

k k k k

# More Lower Case Letters

Here are the rest of the letters. Trace and write them.

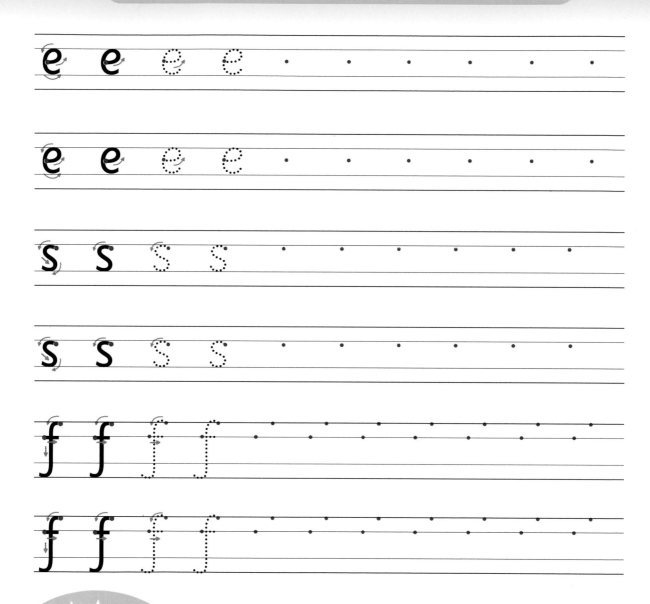

**STAR TIP!**
Look out! These letters don't all work in the same way. But don't worry – start at the dot and follow the arrows and you'll be fine!

8

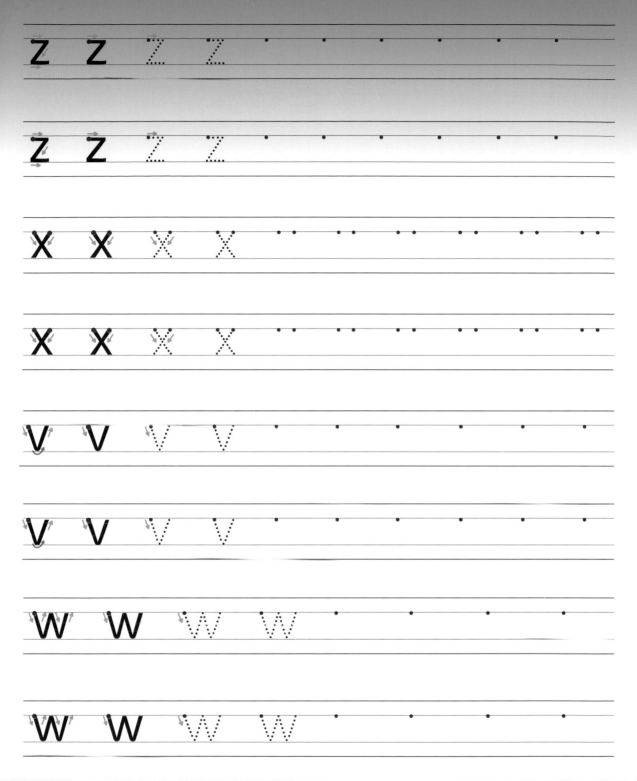

Z Z Z Z

Z Z Z Z

X X X X

X X X X

V V V V

V V V V

W W W W

W W W W

I'm a **wonderful world!**

9

# Starting To Join Letters

Joined-up writing starts here! Trace and write to join these pairs of letters. Don't stop when you've written the first letter – make a diagonal line up to the start of the second letter!

in

tr

dr

mp

ly

al

it

Use the same join to write these words.

pen  pen

bump  bump

drip  drip

sit  sit

a funny pink bunny

a funny pink bunny

11

# Joining More Letters

You're getting good at this! Trace and write to join these pairs of letters too.

ea    ea    ·    ·    ·    ·

ag    ag    ·    ·    ·    ·    ·

nd    nd    ·    ·    ·    ·

do    do    ·    ·    ·    ·

ld    ld    ·    ·    ·    ·    ·

★★★
## STAR TIP!
These joins are like the last ones – but remember to go up to the top of the curve on the second letter, stop, and then go back round to the left. Follow the arrows.
★★★

big big

heal heal

hand hand

cake cake

that bug likes bananas

that bug likes bananas

# More Letters To Join

Here's another way of joining letters. Trace and write to practise these!

oi   oi

ru   ru

ry   ry

wa   wa

ou   ou

vy   vy

STAR TIP!
These letters are joined with a line that goes straight across. Start at the dot and follow the arrows!

**Keep going!**
You're doing really well!

boy boy

home home

win win

love love

a bowl of wavy gravy

a bowl of wavy gravy

# Lots More Joining

You know so many ways of joining letters now! Here are some more to practise.

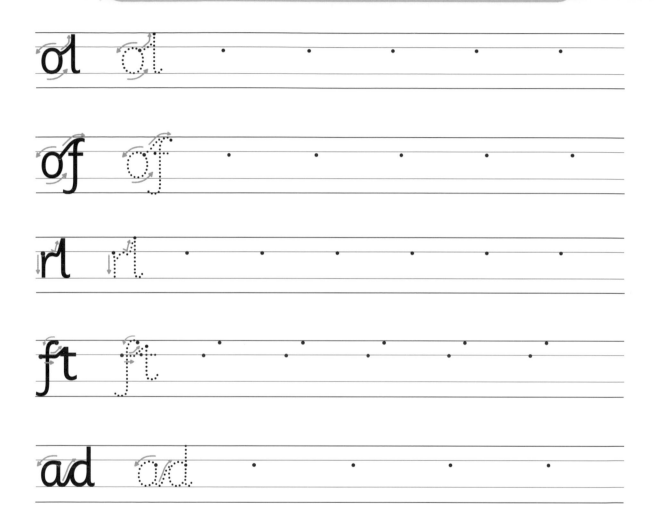

ol

of

rl

ft

ad

## Well done!
You've almost finished learning about joining letters!

### STAR TIP!
Look out – these letters aren't all joined in the same way! Start at the dot and follow the arrows and you'll be fine.

16

wood wood

owl owl

raft raft

fluff fluff

I'm mad about frogs

I'm mad about frogs

# Write The Jokes

What do you call a

peanut in space?

An astro-nut!

What do you call a

peanut in space?

An astro-nut!

18

**STAR TIP!**
Join as many of the letters as you can! If you're not sure how to make a join, look back in the book.

Why did the cow go up

in a rocket?

To see the moooooooon!

Why did the cow go up

in a rocket?

To see the moooooooon!

# Capital Letters

A A   B B   C C   D D

E E   F F   G G   H H

I I   J J   K K   L L

M M   N N   O O   P P

Q Q   R R   S S   T T

U U   V V   W W   X X

Y Y   Z Z